THIS SCARY BOOK BELONGS TO:
_____

trick or treat

Boo Halloween
Activity Book

TRICK OR TREAT

Eve Holiday

Find all 10 differences between these pictures!

WHY ARE VAMPIRES SO EASY TO CHEAT?

Because they're suckers!

It's bedtime! Get Vlad the Vampire to his coffin.

CACKLES AND SCREAMS

Across: →

1. When you're scared you _____.
2. A household pet.
3. Walking bones.
4. What pirates wear.
5. Trick-or-_____!
6. An orange vegetable.

Down: ↓

1. Something that follows you around all day.
7. Where dead people are buried.
8. The sound a witch makes.
9. Where vampires sleep.

Find all 5 differences between these pictures!

#6
WHY AREN'T GHOSTS GOOD AT LYING?

Because you can see right through them!

ALL THINGS HALLOWEEN

```
Z S E G G N F O C T O B E R H C
X T Z S G H O S T V U B Y I C Q
V A P U E X R K A K G S G E T Y
S E G N I K P M U P Q U S M I E
G R O E E G N A R O E A P U W B
M T A C Y G T U S U K T I T B Y
Z H N E E W O L L A H N D S V D
Q D E T N U A H J T W P E O C N
D X O G R A V E Y A R D R C F A
D K Z H J O A U T U M N S Z P C
```

AUTUMN	OCTOBER	SPIDERS
PUMPKIN	COSTUME	CANDY
TREATS	HALLOWEEN	HAUNTED
GRAVEYARD	ORANGE	
WITCH	GHOST	

#8

Unscramble the words found in the picture!

RATS

_ _ _ _

SCALET

_ _ _ _ _ _

DORA

_ _ _ _

THIWE

_ _ _ _ _

REET

_ _ _ _

THIGN

_ _ _ _ _

KNIPPUM

_ _ _ _ _ _ _

SABT

_ _ _ _

Help Mr Mummy find his way out of the scary maze!

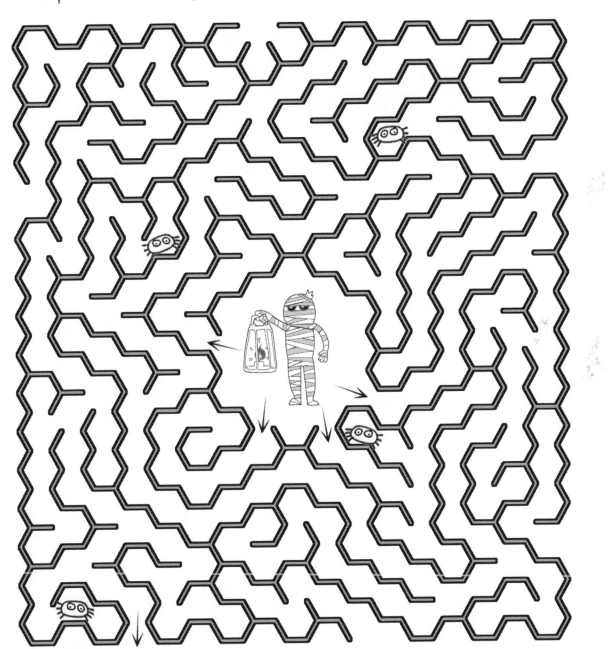

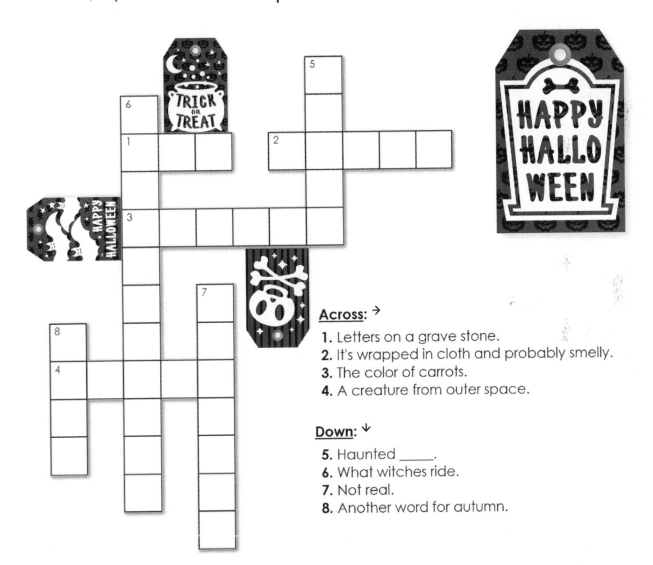

REST IN PEACE

Across: →

1. Letters on a grave stone.
2. It's wrapped in cloth and probably smelly.
3. The color of carrots.
4. A creature from outer space.

Down: ↓

5. Haunted _____.
6. What witches ride.
7. Not real.
8. Another word for autumn.

#12

WHERE DO WIZARDS GO
TO LEARN
NEW SPELLS?

To Wicca-pedia!

Get the ghosts back to the haunted house!

#13

Find all 7 differences between these pictures!

CHILLING WORDS

```
W C G H H T I J T F
J A B E K R F C W X
F Y E O O G D H N Q
Y J S G G C B A C P
P S O H B C U B H B
E N C R O S Z G I L
E I F A E C Y I L O
R I R O R J K W L O
C A U E L Y D I I D
Z S P N E M K G N Y
T I N G L I N G G G
Y R O G I H C P I E
C I W R Y K O O P S
L N L B D R N U T H
K U G R I M F B N G
W B I Z A R R E O C
```

CREEPY
TINGLING
SHOCKING
BLOODY
GOOEY
CHILLING
BIZARRE
GRIM
NAUSEOUS
SPOOKY
GORY
SCARY
EERIE

It's time to go, Neko!

WHAT DID THE
    BUTCHER SAY TO THE
        BAD ZOMBIE?

You're
dead
meat!

Unscramble the words found in the picture!

SOCLUD

_ _ _ _ _ _

RHON

_ _ _ _

DOWWIN

_ _ _ _ _ _

LUPPER

_ _ _ _ _ _

HETET

_ _ _ _ _

NOMO

_ _ _ _

BYESALLE

_ _ _ _ _ _ _ _

SMORTEN

_ _ _ _ _ _ _

Find all 10 differences between these pictures!

BLOODY SPIDERS

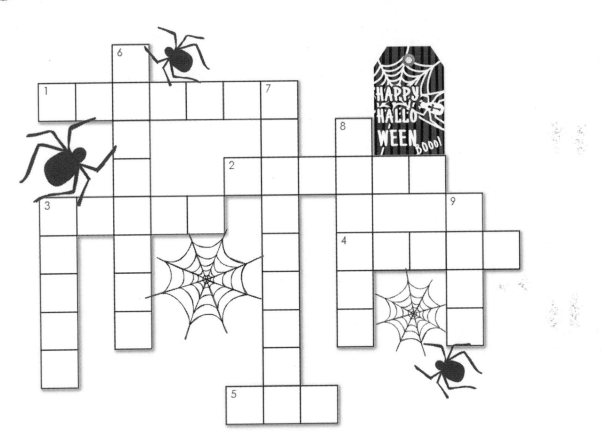

Across: →

1. They make webs.
2. Another word for scary.
3. _____-or-treat!
4. Red liquid.
5. What ghosts say to scare you.

Down: ↓

3. A creature that lives under a bridge.
6. 12am.
7. Batman is a _____.
8. A monster that eats people's brains.
9. It's white and round in the night sky.

#21

WHAT DO BATS
LIKE TO DO IN THEIR
FREE TIME?

Swing

dance!

Help Mama bat find her baby!

Find all 6 differences between these pictures!

NAME A KIND OF SANDWICH YOU CAN'T EAT.

A sand witch!

Unscramble the words found in the picture!

CAPCUKE

_ _ _ _ _ _ _

THA

_ _ _

CYAND

_ _ _ _ _

OMSWR

_ _ _ _ _

ROBOM

_ _ _ _ _

DANCEL

_ _ _ _ _ _

LOW

_ _ _

SAGLESS

_ _ _ _ _ _ _

#26

CREEPY COSTUMES

```
x  j  p  u  h  f  l  o  w  e  r  e  w  f  c
s  g  h  o  u  l  v  n  k  r  y  z  r  a  g
x  n  q  s  w  n  a  e  m  d  y  e  l  l  y
j  m  o  a  y  m  m  u  m  x  k  i  f  i  j
w  r  e  t  q  l  p  t  f  a  c  b  q  e  l
u  e  k  q  e  r  i  z  t  m  p  m  r  n  n
s  a  m  w  n  l  r  r  y  l  o  o  d  t  a
i  p  n  n  t  d  e  z  k  n  k  z  b  s  m
q  e  k  q  w  d  z  k  m  y  j  m  d  w  y
i  r  i  y  n  o  t  l  s  d  e  b  e  q  e
b  l  f  u  q  c  l  t  p  p  b  y  v  v  g
z  o  k  r  y  g  l  c  k  q  o  t  i  g  o
n  k  i  m  j  m  o  t  n  a  h  p  l  o  b
```

clown
zombie
phantom
alien
vampire
werewolf
ghoul
bogeyman
mummy
undertaker
devil
skeleton
reaper

This little devil needs his pitchfork. Help him find it!

#28

GHOSTS AND GRAVEYARDS

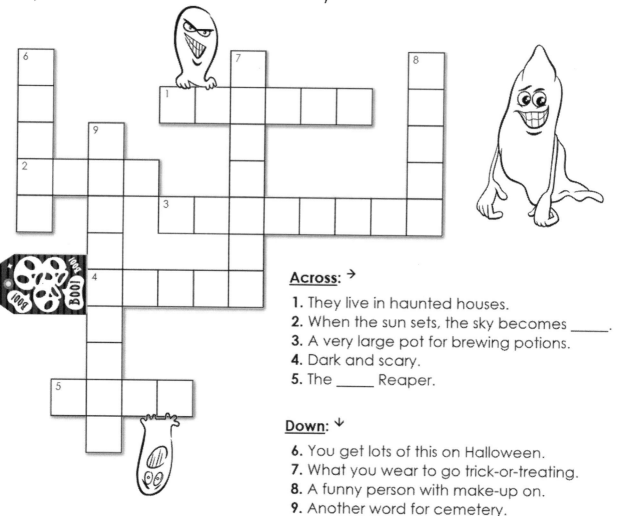

Across: →

1. They live in haunted houses.
2. When the sun sets, the sky becomes _____.
3. A very large pot for brewing potions.
4. Dark and scary.
5. The _____ Reaper.

Down: ↓

6. You get lots of this on Halloween.
7. What you wear to go trick-or-treating.
8. A funny person with make-up on.
9. Another word for cemetery.

Find all 5 differences between these pictures!

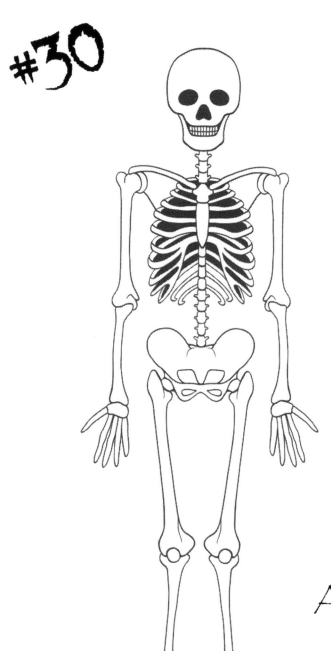

HOW MUCH DOES A SKELETON WEIGH?

A skele-TONNE!

Help Frankie find a new hand!

#32
SCARY THINGS

```
U D X E E L O A R T J M A S K
F P X N Y U E V S P A I V O B
Q S Z O E C N K C S P K V P W
K W P T B L U I C I C R R P M
B J T S A L P N O I T O P I J
X F E B L T B I T Y V T N T C
J Y K M L S G S Y E G G M C O
A I B O S Y M Q U B O P O H F
W K B T K O F R V J K S W F F
X I B L O O D P L C M T Q O I
L N O R D L U A C E X C J R N
P C B Y X A U I V U R G G K B
V K V Z M M K H K Q L I C A W
V Q W B D R F A N G S Q W S Y
W Y C Q R R K E N O B I B J N
```

EYEBALLS

BLOOD

FOG

SKULL

POTION

FANGS

BROOMSTICK

MASK

TOMBSTONE

CAULDRON

PITCHFORK

BONE

COFFIN

Find all 8 differences between these pictures!

#34
Unscramble the words found in the picture!

CEFEN
_ _ _ _ _

COWSCARER
_ _ _ _ _ _ _ _

YIMNECH
_ _ _ _ _ _ _

GRANOE
_ _ _ _ _ _

HOGST
_ _ _ _ _

CLABTACK
_ _ _ _ _ _ _ _

CHARNB
_ _ _ _ _ _

BEWISPERD
_ _ _ _ _ _ _ _ _

NIGHTMARE PARTY

Across: →

1. Another word for costume.
2. A hole in the ground for dead bodies.
3. A celebration with food and drinks.
4. The sound a wolf makes.

Down: ↓

5. A tool that helps you see in the dark.
6. Witches and warlocks can use _____.
7. A scary dream.
8. Halloween is in _____.
9. Another word for ghost.

#36

WHAT DO BIRDS DO ON HALLOWEEN NIGHT?

They go
twick-or tweeting!

Skellie needs her candy! Help her get to them.

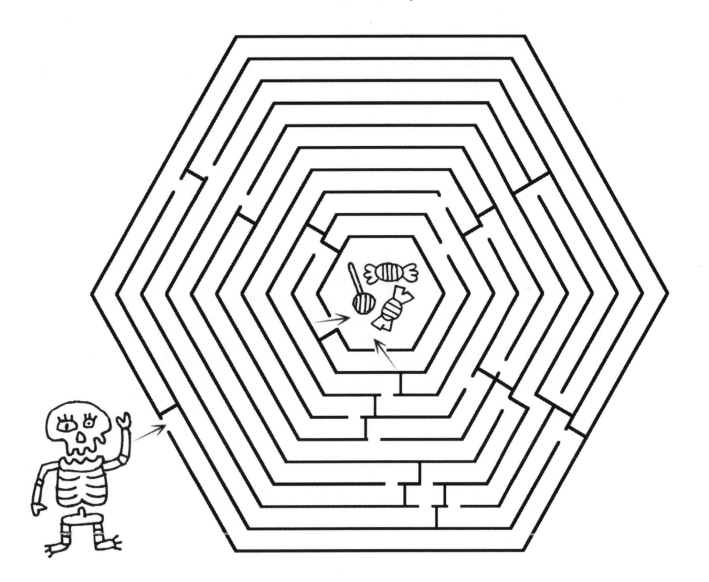

#38

Find all 7 differences between these pictures!

WHAT'S THAT SOUND?

```
n t n o q s c u t r q r
d s c r e e c h x l s r
h k a e r c b a n g q w
m t r e h t i l s h w b
l w o h t z s b i g y o
c s n h u a z q b u g o
a d x t a f v m o a i l
c r e v i h s a v l s s
k l m l a j c e n h r n
l i p h i s s r o p v d
e a l p c s w c x j o k
j w a z a j k s k r o q
```

cackle	screech	bang
boo	wail	shiver
scream	shock	laugh
hiss	howl	
creak	slither	

#40

Help unite the two friends!

WHAT'S THE OPPOSITE OF A MUMMY?

A duddy!

#41

#42
Unscramble the words found in the picture!

VEGAR

_ _ _ _ _

RAGSS

_ _ _ _ _

ROWC

_ _ _ _

JOCKATERNNAL

_ _ _ _ ' _ ' _ _ _ _ _

STRAS

_ _ _ _ _

SETSUN

_ _ _ _ _ _

SHAND

_ _ _ _ _

WHY ARE SOME BIRDS AFRAID OF HAUNTED HOUSES?

Because they are chicken!

Wendy lost her witch's hat. Help her find it!

Find all 6 differences between these pictures!

Coloring Books

Check out these other favorite holiday books!

29

#38

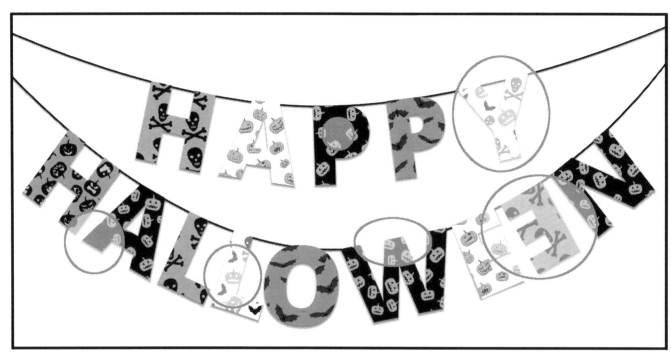

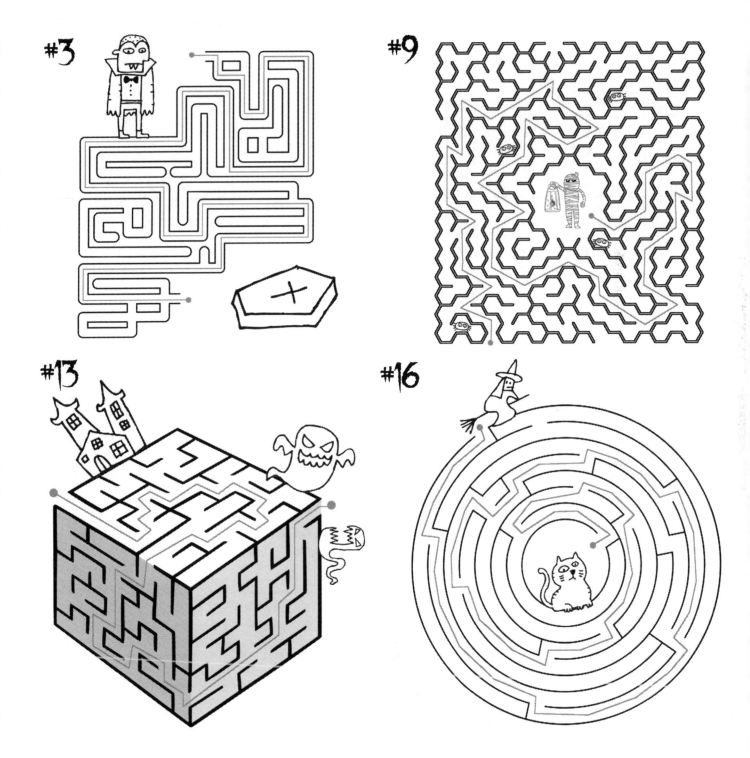

#3

#9

#13

#16

#22

#27

#31

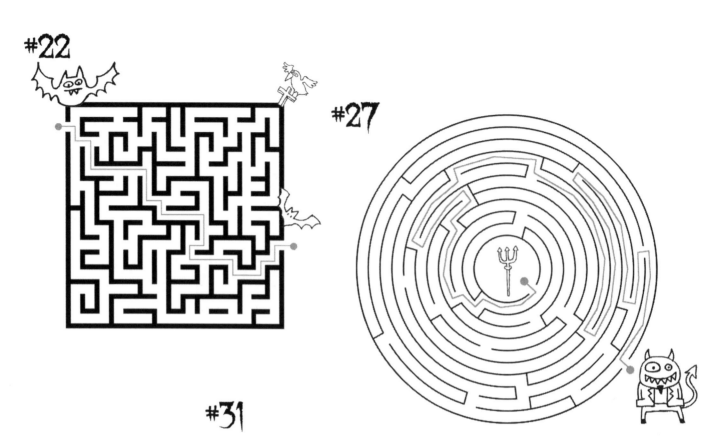

#37

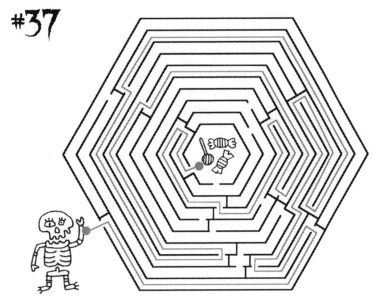

#40

#44

#4 CACKLES AND SCREAMS

Across and Down entries:

- SCREAM
- CAT
- CACKLE
- SHADOW
- CEMETERY
- SKELETON
- EYEPATCH
- COFFIN
- TREAT
- PUMPKIN

#11 REST IN PEACE

- HOUSE
- BROOMSTICKS
- RIP
- MUMMY
- ORANGE
- FANTASY
- FALL
- ALIENS

#20 BLOODY SPIDERS

- MIDNIGHT
- SPIDERS
- SUPERHERO
- TROLL
- TRICK
- SPOOKY
- ZOMBIE
- BLOOD
- MOON
- BOO

#28 GHOSTS AND GRAVEYARDS

Crossword answers:

- CANDY
- DARK
- GHOSTS
- COSTUME
- CLOWN
- GRAVEYARD
- CAULDRON
- EERIE
- GRIM

#35 NIGHTMARE PARTY

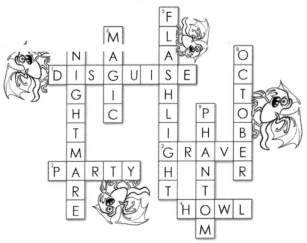

Crossword answers:

- MAGIC
- FLASHLIGHT
- NIGHTMARE
- DISGUISE
- OCTOBER
- PHANTOM
- PARTY
- GRAVE
- HOWL

#7 ALL THINGS HALLOWEEN

```
Z S E G G N F O C T O B E R H C
X T Z S G H O S T V U B Y I C Q
V A P U E X R K A K G S G E T Y
S E G N I K P M U P Q U S M I E
G R O E E G N A R O E A P U W B
M T A C Y G T U S U K T I T B Y
Z H N E E W O L L A H N D S V D
Q D E T N U A H J T W P E O C N
D X O G R A V E Y A R D R C F A
D K Z H J O A U T U M N S Z P C
```

#15 CHILLING WORDS

```
W C G H H T I J T F
J A B E K R F C W X
F Y E O O G D H N Q
Y J S G G C B A C P
P S O H B C U B H B
E N C R O S Z G I L
E I F A E C Y I L O
R I R O R J K W L O
C A U E L Y D I I D
Z S P N E M K G N Y
T I N G L I N G G G
Y R O G I H C P I E
C I W R Y K O O P S
L N L B D R N U T H
K U G R I M F B N G
W B I Z A R R E O C
```

#26 CREEPY COSTUMES

```
x j p u h f l o w e r e w f c
s g h o u l v n k r y z r a g
x n q s w n a e m d y e l l y
j m o a y m m u m x k i f i j
w r e t q l p t f a c b q e l
u e k q e r i z t m p m r n n
s a m w n l r r y l o o d t a
i p n n t d e z k n k z b s m
q e k q w d z k m y j m d w y e
i r i y n o t l s d e b e q e
b l f u q c l t p p b y v g
z o k r y g l c k q o t i g o
n k i m j m o t n a h p l o b
```

#32 SCARY THINGS

```
U D X E E L O A R T J M A S K
F P X N Y U E V S P A I V O B
Q S Z O E C N K C S P K V P W
K W P T B L U I C I C R R P M
B J T S A L P N O I T O P I J
X F E B L T B I T Y V T N T C
J Y K M L S G Y E G G M C O
A I B O S Y M Q U B O P O H F
W K B T K O F R V J K S W F F
X I B L O O D P L C M T Q O I
L N O R D L U A C E X C J R N
P C B Y X A U I V U R G G K B
V K V Z M M K H K Q L I C A W
V Q W B D R F A N G S Q W S Y
W Y C Q R R K E N O B I B J N
```

#39 WHAT'S THAT SOUND?

```
n t n o q s c u t r q r
d s c r e e c h x l s r
h k a e r c b a n g q w
m t r e h t i l s h w b
l w o h t z s b i g y o
c s n h u a z q b u g o
a d x t a f v m o a i l
c r e v i h s a v l s s
k l m l a j c e n h r n
l i p h i s s r o p v d
e a l p c s w c x j o k
j w a z a j k s k r o q
```

#8 star, castle, road

white, tree

night, pumpkin, bats

#18 clouds, horn, window

purple, teeth

moon, eye balls, monster

#25 cupcake, hat, candy

worms, broom

candle, owl, glasses

#34 fence, scarecrow, chimney

orange, ghost

black cat, branch, spider web

#42 grave, grass

crow, jack-o'-lantern, stars

sunset, hands

Made in the USA
Lexington, KY
26 September 2018